SUNLIGHT FRAGMENTS

SUNLIGHT FRAGMENTS

Poems by Don L. Nickerson

PENNYWYSE
PRESS
TUCSON, ARIZONA

Copyright © 2009 by Don Nickerson

All rights reserved. No part of this book may be reproduced or transmitted in any form or by any means, electronic or mechanical, including photocopying, recording or by any information storage and retrieval system, without written permission from the author, except for the inclusion of a brief quotation in a review.

Published in the United States of America by:

Pennywyse Press
3710 East Edison Street
Tucson, AZ 85716

LCCN 2009940904

ISBN 978-1-935437-12-3
ISBN 1-935437-12-7

Book and Cover Design by Leila Joiner
Front cover photo: light falls on corals with many coral fish © kristian sekulic
Back cover photo: underwater © Nat Ulrich

Printed in the United States of America on Acid-Free Paper

Grateful acknowledgement to the following publications in which these poems have previously appeared or will soon appear:

The Deronda Review, "Hard Drive, Your Aging Face"

Empty Vessel, "Old Men Laughing," "We Meet Again Each Day"

Fireweed, "General Arugula," "Holiday," "My Father Headed In"

Hubbub, "For Li Po"

The Laughing Dog, "Benjamin Franklin Visits China," "If I Were A Chinese Poet," "Ocean Barges"

The Penwood Review, "Remembering A Friend"

The Rockford Review, "Secret Agent"

The Write Word, "Coffee At Doña Luisa's"

The Veil, "Dangerous Bridges"

This book of poems is dedicated to my four children, who have much to do with creating them and the writer:

Lynn Susan Davis, David Lawrence Nickerson, Karen Lee Ludwig, and Katherine Ann Dunkley

CONTENTS

I Connections
Zen Poetry on a Plane to Chicago
Waving at the Engineer
Secret Agent
This Body
Remembering a Friend
Three Moths and a Red Leather Chair
Whale Consciousness
We Meet Again Each Day

II Other Places
If I were a Chinese Poet
Old Men Laughing
Benjamin Franklin Visits China
For Li Po
Beyond the White Pagoda
Coffee at Doña Luisa's
The Prison
Seasons
Torremolinos

III Aging
Suspense
Meditation on Getting Old
Dishwasher at Eventide
Garter Snakes
This Moment
Just One Thought Away
Yellow Petals
Same Old, Same Old

IV Spirit

    Kick the Can
    Man Made of Straw
    Swamp Light
    Hard Drive
    Ocean Barges
    Wisdom
    Swami Rami
    Mostly Happy
    Forgery Expert

V Love

    You are Not an Orphan
    My Father Headed In
    Your Aging Face
    Blue Checkbook
    The Cheater
    Wishing You Joy
    Speaking of Love
    Waterfall and Pool
    Letter to Li Po
    Holiday

VI Fun

    Hurryin' Up To Get my Beer
    Dangerous Bridges
    General Arugula

Postscript

I

Connections

Zen Poetry on a Plane to Chicago

On the plane to Chicago I open my
age-faded book of Zen poems and

Turn to an inscription from my wife:
For Don with love, Linda, May, 1983.

Outside the window clouds roll past like
a zoo train carrying Buddhas.

Wishing the hot coffee would come,
I bite into a chocolate chip cookie,

Swirl pieces about with my tongue.
Decaf, please, with cream and sugar.

I stir and sip my coffee, watch more clouds,

Imagine the plane to be a flying turtle
sheltering a thousand secret love affairs.

Only an old man thinks this way
who reads too much Zen,

Traces with his fingers
fading words of love.

Waving at the Engineer

My father was turned down when he volunteered for
World War II after he had been a naval telegrapher
in the first war, but he would stand in front of his yellow
clapboard station and wave when trains loaded with
field guns exploded through our dusty little desert town.

I thought he had something to do with winning our war,
his fierce eagle countenance and determined wave, so
like his belief he could cure my mother of tuberculosis
when she was seventeen, moving them from Dubuque,
Iowa, to the Mojave Desert in California. He treated her

With a folk cure of eggs and whiskey and she made it.
Held together by such faith we felt obliged to survive.
Telegraph operator, agent, healer, house builder, lover of
flowers and birds, smoker of Pall Malls and Lucky Strikes.

Through the window of our passenger train headed for
Seattle I see two fishermen down by a river. They lift up
their poles toward us and the engineer sends back two throaty
whistles, a secret code that I, and all children, understand.

When a man playing on a golf course jabs his club in the air
as we pass I remember the Santa Fe calendars on our wall,
Navajo Indians in full dress raising feathered spears, and I think
of myself in World War II, a company guide-on bearer,

Driving a blue flag toward the sky for all the weary men behind at the end of a 20-mile march in July: We're in sight of the promised land and the taste of cold beers. They cheer.

The train whistle blows for an approaching small town crossing, its sound cradled in morning mist. Children's faces lean out windows from waiting cars. They wave their arms back and forth, the way I waved goodbye to my father the day I buried him.

Secret Agent

I am often unaware
I have a secret countenance
until a passerby nods or grins
unaccountably, or my wife
may ask, "Why are you
smiling?" when I never know
I am. After all, I can't just
blurt out, I have a rogue
agent inside me!

Sometimes walking down a
street I will spy my reflection
in a glass and expect to catch
a frown coming back
unawares, but it is always
the same surprise,

myself in disguise,
looking back amused.

This Body

This body
a bleach wrinkled canvas
stretching into some gale
that could deliver it from melancholy
groaning in favor of unknown edges

This body
yearning for a home
in the empty place
behind a watchful navel

This body
profane temple made of pocked stones
put together with bullets, dust and acid rain
inside-outside seared by fire, redeemed by water

This body
streaming
electric just as Blake said
killers doing perfidious deeds
circuits of lovers
circuits of friends

all living things
This body

Remembering a Friend

for Doug…
    for Bill

I once thought my wife held the only goddess,
behind the veil of her blue-green eyes,
but when I saw my dying friend's snot

Drip into the folds of the bed's white sheets
there was a goddess again and my eyes teared.
My friend's heart was one thing I'd like to own,

Though he told me my heart beats strong, too.
If there are things we regard highly on our way,
let a good heart be sought above all other,

a gate still swinging or left ajar, no one in sight.

When the skies are bold and dark, I ask of him,
Don't drift so far away in my universe that I
cannot point and say, there he is, the bright star

Mid-way, his the star I will always see.

When I was out walking and met a stranger
in an open space, he said not a word to me,
at the dew-filled meadow beneath a

Weeping Willow tree. He wet my boots with
moss and grass, covered my back with fallen leaves,
and in that state of reassuring peace

I fell sound asleep.

Moths and a Red Leather Chair

—for Lynn

680 miles they'd come
    a trip that began early
  my oldest daughter and her fiancé rolling up
    in a sleek rig too beautiful
      to be called a pickup
        but that's what it was,
          a lumpy tarp laid out in back.
My wife of two years and I hurried to greet them,
   drew back when two heads popped out
     from the tarp,
       one dark the other fair,
         thin arms and legs following,
    two young daughters screaming
    Surprise! Surprise!
They reached out their arms to find us and
    fell against our welling tears.

I used to tell myself about those two they're gone, gone,
   to make life easier,
     but at night memories rose up
       like dark waters
         and spilled their edges.

I'm lucky to have a strong birth-child
    who made life better for a father
      than it might have been,
      beautiful many-hued moth
        who believes in light,
      guiding her younger sisters to a
        reading lamp
          beside a red leather chair.

Whale Consciousness

I will tell you a truth the whale could share
    with us if we were awake,
A consciousness that we belong to the sea
    and all that is there,
Not something the whale thinks about,
    strives to achieve,
        just what *is*,
The whale, and all of us, One.

It is the secret reason we try to kill it,
Why Moby Dick is about war between
    ego and Being,
The ego's drive for control,
    its rationalizations for survival.

But when the killing is done
    and blood fills the seas
        when the ego feels its emptiness,
And fails to understand,
    it goes out to kill again to fill it.

You know who you are, don't you,
    who a whale is?
Your dance is playing itself out among the waves.
    The leviathan soars,
        carries you on its back.

We Meet Once Again Each Day[1]

We will be far away
but you will come to us
at our practice of Qigong,
and we will come to you
as a fish swims the great sea.

We part, it is true,
yet to meet again each day
at the feathered tips
of our outstretched wings,
and under the sturdy arms
of the cedar tree.

The teacher is in *bai hui*,
The teacher is in *dan tian*
and *lao gong*.
You cannot be far away
Professor Chen Fu-yin.
You cannot be very far away,
Master Chen.
You are in the Qi
that enters the gate of our heart.

We take leave of one another,
but look! look!
Look at the golden moon
how it rises
just behind the Buddha's head!

---

[1] This poem was written for the final banquet of faculty, staff, and students in the "Qigong in China" program, August 10-26, 1994, conducted by the Chinese Academy of Somatic Sciences, Beijing, China.

II

OTHER PLACES

If I Were a Chinese Poet

O, to write like Li-Po or Han-Shan!
I would make poem after poem, a stream
and its cool spray for our summer faces.

If I could write like Tu-Fu my children
would hold their faces and grin through
fingered spaces. They would take my poems

and hide them in secret places where they
could begin to dream words of their own
and write them in cloth and leather diaries.

If I were a Chinese Poet I would write poems
for my wife which had come to me in the night
and shyly read them to her at breakfast.

This morning, warmed by the sun, and stirred
by imaginings, it does not matter I am as old
as a creaky gate, or that I can no longer

climb mountains, drink wine after sunset.
It does not even matter that I am not Chinese.
Honored guests at my table, they nod as I write.

Old Men Laughing

Young people here in Beijing still think
they can change the world.
It is the same old thing: passion,
ideals, beliefs…all the usual afflictions
of youth.

But in reality I have seen how young men
pedal up our road before dawn
their wooden platforms five feet long
and jutting out a foot on either side,
loaded down with slabs of beef
or produce from farms,
sometimes a wife
or two children asleep,
Occasionally rotting garbage.

They lean their thin bodies,
left, right, left, right,
and they pass by young women growing
old in just a few weeks as they bend
their pitched shawls into mustard fields.

Why, then, do clumps of old men
laugh at night under one bare light bulb
while they play games and gossip?
And why do the old women giggle
when they invite us to join them
at morning Qigong in Jingshan Park?

What is it they share
with their impassioned grandchildren
that I fail to comprehend?

August, 1994

Benjamin Franklin Visits China

A copper penny glistens after an early
morning storm but no one bothers.

Shamelessly I bend to pluck it
from the gutter with my left hand.

Eleven O'clock in the morning,
already an omen of good fortune.

For Li Po

An empty bottle
Nothing stands between the winds
and the wild waving bamboo

Wishes for other seasons
fly away like curled leaves
A thousand birds peck away

At the old thatched roof
while a single gray shutter is loose
bangs and bangs like a jubilant child

It is a day like midnight
clouds dark as grief
passing through amber

And back out again
Corks lie about everywhere

Beyond the White Pagoda

My love is far away
   beyond the white pagoda
      and the white capped sea

With my mind I do not think of her
   though sometimes I do not tell
      the truth about such things

One day in Beijing I opened a small jeweled
   box in my heart and found her face
      looking back
         morning tide of Tai Chi
            Qigong master healer
      holding my left shoulder
         in her two hands
ocean finding empty spaces in the sands

Tonight
   yellow moon shines
      through willow's
         folded wings
   pebbled courtyard stays asleep
   I alone am awake
      watch golden beams caress
         the green paint window sill

Coffee at Doña Luisa's

Antígua, Guatemala, is not a place to be troubled by death,
or a 13 year old girl flipping tortillas while she cradles the
head of her sprawled out, drunken husband with her other arm.
This is the place to buy property, the smartly dressed ones say.

The temperature is mild, seldom varying more than ten degrees.
Breathtaking purple and red bougainvillea crawl up and over
limestone walls topped with broken colored pieces of glass
embedded in cement, meant to slash and discourage thieves.

Impressive 17th century Cathedrals, monasteries, convents and
building ruins are everywhere, bordered by cobblestone streets.
Even devastating earthquake ruins sell history and properties.
Artisans at La Iglésia de San Francisco recreate Moorish filigree.

But at night, Indian men, women and children wind down
ancient paths into the city out of the red-rich scrub pine hills.
They pick their way through familiar broken monastery stones,
hunt for places to relieve themselves and curl up in sleep.

In the foothills edging the city suffering erupts, skeletons
emerge from shallow graves. Some skeletons become children
who sell their mother's sweat in city parks next day, glistening
beads of sweat that cling to bright shawls tourists buy cheap.

The smallest children chew on mangoes and never seem to cry.
It's part of the charm of colorful Antígua. A good time to buy.
Our language school tells us violence here is no worse than in
Chicago or Cleveland, but word gets around at Doña Luísa's.

Our language school's van was intercepted this week on the way to Cobán. Everyone was robbed: money, jewelry and rings, even their wedding rings. Just outside the city, a Dutch woman student from a different language school was stripped and slain last week.

At Doña Luísa's Coffee House, two doors down from a bank where two men with machine guns stand guard outside, three blocks from Antigua's most celebrated Cathedral, we drink coffee. We huddle together, touch one another, and say "Yes, Yes."

The Prison

There is no place to hide from the imprisoned.
I live in this village after all and I can hear
their chains at night. I see them pull at their
beards, these bent children, muttering as they

pace out their stories into the bleak gray stones,
sniffing at insanity as if it were oil of lavender.
I frequently arouse the idea that if I could
understand these old children there might be a

kind of salvation for them and me. So I read
their files, monotonous medical paragraphs
circumscribed exactly to a couple of pages of
yellow paper for each. Of course, reading never

does any good. The ways in which the prisoners
and I are attached, the ways in which their
mysteries persist, are never affected by my reading.
But I think I still believe that one day the bleak

hurried black script on yellow pages will begin to
smolder, the prisoner's stories will burst into
flames and become red ashes, I will poke
and stir their last remains into revelation.

Seasons

SPRING Oh, spring, you are wild and frisky,
full of yourself in lush green blouses
skirts and hats, but don't forget
where you came from your wily lean
parents their stark raw limbs.

SUMMER Outside my window a scrub pine throws
her body to the dance, her bared breasts
daring a salty wind press against my
nakedness, and she shakes and twirls

her needled castanets held high above
sweat-covered limbs, whirls and spins
past the edges of green bush troubadours,
dazzling pirouette of a scaled gray scrub.

FALL The ebb tide of summer slinks away
driven by late September's squall,
grasps fallen auburn leaves from
a frosted beach, shapes them into

WINTER briny revelries dressed for winter,
light and color becoming burning
musk, splashed into fading dusk.

Torremolinos

As I walk the beach well past midnight
the yellow moon duels with a thousand lights
along the boardwalk at Torremolinos.

Could the memory of tonight outlast the universe
and be plucked from the cosmic stream like a fish,
when I cannot remember my library password?

When I have forgotten the headings of folders
in my files where I have stored my importance?
My past is crumbling like a lesser sphinx.

Is it possible to warn those you love how death
comes about unexpectedly when the last bottle
of pomegranate juice has been stolen from the pantry?

My children may not understand I am too old
to bring back gifts of sagacity and wisdom.

What I offer them are wet smells of the ocean
inside the cuffs of my pants, little more.

III

Aging

Suspense

When we are gone we are gone
some say. Or does time still snare
us after death, shrinking our histories
into prune pits, egos into paint dots?

There will be a Day of Reckoning,
some say. I imagine mine to be stark
as the inside of an empty Cheerios box.
So many great teachers, so much water
spilled careening down rock-strewn hills.

Peering into gray cardboard space I see
scores of plastic cubes whirling through
cosmic streams, miniatures painted in fall
Appalachian colors that define my life:

Two worn track shoes, the left heel spiked,
a tiny onion skin bible, microfilms of a
white clapboard New England church,
a book of calligraphy poems by Tu Fu,

a disk of complaints by my former wives,
a card with mixed grades from my children,

a finely crafted wooden box containing

    nothing but echoes

Meditation on Getting Old

Once out of bed I wobble to my desk
to put books away—poetry, one from
Spain, the other from the Chinese.

They all talk of death the same way,
a sad acceptance, youth the lively kiss
a memory, youth these fresh bodies

And dazzling smiles want the stage.
Who says wrinkles are the cumulative
bank account of wisdom and character?

They are signs of how we disappear.
I don't hate my age. Much of the time
it is a blissful tone of relief acknowledging

My day is done, my work on earth ended.
But I understand, there is a time for all things.
I would like to spend my days like a leaf,

Or a grain of sand, picked up and carried
across the road and landing on an
unsuspecting carefree young man or

Wherever I'm supposed to be, then I wouldn't
feel compelled to strive or figure out any more
priorities, or to make every minute count, as

They say, because any of them could be my last.
I could just get picked up and carried about,
more aware of the sun and gentle wind than

Where I might be going.

Would it be possible to live this way in old age,
if I could imagine my lanky body rearranged,
sensitive in my skin to the whirling wind,

Yielding my heart to yes, yes?

Dishwasher at Eventide

You are so profane
    dishwasher in the kitchen,
      your pishes and pashes flushes
        and rushes,

Yet, amidst the noise
    I hear
      the familiar sound of
        chanting monks.
O, brothers, I have missed you so,
    welcome to my eventide hearth.

The hearing aid in my right ear,
    celebrates your prayers,
      head to the right
        your chants soar
          from a corner of the wall,
      head to the left
        your rumbling bass
          disappears.

Flusher, rusher, washer of dishes
    pots and pans,
      you grip my brother's fates
        in the blue fingers
          of your trays.

But I say,
    chant on brothers!
      defying soapy rivers,
        rains of peas and rice
      the pishes,
        the click-click-click.

Garter Snakes

In one corner of our cluttered kitchen
drawer there are two piles of wire stays
that once held together bunches of carrots
and red-leaf chard. They lie there like

sleeping baby garter snakes separated by
lengths. Aware of my inability to throw
away even one, I am compelled to ask for
the first time: is this what death looks like

at last, far more wire stays in a drawer
than I have left of years? Is death in books
I will never read that wince from their tight
shelves, or stacks of magazines I hide from,

stacking them next to cellophane-wrapped
rolls of toilet paper in dark, moaning closets?
I look around and find more potent statements
I am still alive: travel bags, jaunty blue caps,

six pair of white, alternating tennis shoes that
stand at attention and wait for my command.
Still, how long will these symbols stay alive?
Some balance between the illusion of endless

time and the reality of endings seems good.
But first I must find the courage to reach
inside a kitchen drawer and pull out all but
ten of the little garter snakes sleeping there.

Do Not Let This Day Pass

—for Linda

Do not let this day pass into night
    without looking at her body,
        the flesh of her thigh
        the fine tone of her skin,

Look fully with your eyes and not
    from some ideal your head
    tells your eyes they should see.

I dare you, look anywhere on her body,
    a knee perhaps, a single toe,
    or her face. Trace the lines of her
        wrinkles as if your eyes
        were your loving fingers.

See where there is a sag here and there,
places where the skin may have
become spotty, almost the color
and texture of parchment.

See, in all this looking, if you are not
> looking at the very same skin
> from 25 years ago, 50 years ago.
>> It is the same skin as your
>> lover, your bride, skin you
> love because she has always been
> your treasure.

Do not let this day pass into night without
> looking into her eyes. Let them rest
> there, as if each of you were drinking
>> from a deep, pure stream.
>> There is no effort, like a horse
> dropping its head to drink from a river.

You cannot hold back time. It will pass in
> spite of you and even through you.
> You cannot hold back mortality,
>> which is a child of time.

But do not let this day pass into the night
> without looking, while there is still light.

Just One Thought Away

It occurred to me one day
I am just one thought away
    from oblivion
The thought I had yesterday
    didn't stay
The one I had today I can't
    remember

When the master advises us
    to cultivate a mind
    of not knowing
I find it not difficult
    my mind a rolled up
    toothpaste tube

Nothing left to squeeze

Yellow Petals

I am learning how to be nothing,
    to drift with sand and awaken
        to the songs of catalpa leaves.

At night, when my hands seize up,
    I whisper to them in their sleep,
    be still, be at peace.

Nevertheless my dreams ask when?
When will my loneliness end?

When will I become so transparent
    life flows through the fine mesh
    of my beginnings.

When will a rain of loosened yellow
    petals fall on my nodding head?

Same Old, Same Old

It is the same old I,
    sore neck,
        stomach complaints,

Yet I smile
    at how the seaweed sways
    and dances inside.

IV

Spirit

Kick the Can

I was the can in God's game of
      "Kick the Can"
until one night He picked me up
out of the street and said it's over.

I pondered over the years what
He meant by that and I decided
I was not the can not the kicker

Just part of the game late at night
underneath a bug-yellow hazed light
hiding until mother called me home.

Man Made of Straw

I have come to appreciate
those "goddamn fundamentalists,"
and their barbed wire fences
to hold in the sheep,
    their peaceful mentalities munching,
        waiting for judgment day,
            when the rest of us will
            get ours.

He is returning in glory, they say,
lowering down into the fields
and yelling out, Come! Come!
to all the curled white beasts.
Come!
    and suddenly they lift up as one
    to meet Jesus at 300 feet,
    about the height at which
    a parachute must open
    for anyone who might be
    on the way down instead.

Then they are gone, this ascending throng
of white wool and black hooves,
    we hear the sound of choral music,
    sweeter than angels, amazingly similar
    to the erotically tainted voice of
    Aunt Zelda when she sang in the choir.

I have come to appreciate fundamentalists,
    their baling wire hope,
        because life is hard for all of us,
            wanting to love, but finding so many
                small pools of acid in our brains,

and I, like so many, am a man made of straw,
wondering which part of me will blow away next,
    what could be left underneath my checkered
    blue shirt and denim pants when the blackbirds
        have settled in.

So why not creeds,
    black leather bibles waved from meaty hands?
Why not the words of Jesus underlined in red?
This is, after all, an awesome fissure we are in
    and I have come to appreciate
        what arrogance is required
            to live or die,
how strong the rope must be to winch us up.

Swamp Light

Light is what I believe in.
What else is there when Fall,
naked and dying, bares it limbs

for Winter, when I feel an ache
in my side where I once gave up
God for the sake of light?

The light I believe in has no mass
at all. It lies beneath acres of moss,
incandescence, groaning into frogs and fish

Hard Drives

It isn't sleep I need
    it's deliverance
from my hard drives.

I long for the peace
    of God
that only love can bring

Ocean Barge

I have a Bible in my home,
   a Buddha and the Qur'an.
I have St. Theresa
   and the Upanishads,
     not to mention the Bhagavadgita.

I have so much religion in my hold
   I may capsize,
     I may never die,
       just age and age,
        and finally like a tired old barge,
         break apart,

boilerplates and stacks
   sinking,
     dispersing themselves all about
      the ocean floor,
    bubbling for all the visitors,
      the flat and funny fish.

Wisdom

In a younger life people mistook my silence
for hidden wisdom and never guessed silence
hid shame.

In reality I was swinging from one trapeze
bar to another through the endless night
we call life,

Asking to be noticed while staying invisible.

My trick of illusions is reaching its apex in old age.
I experience peace, a sleight of forgetfulness,

Not remembering bad dreams on my morning walk
up the graveled path, past the tremulous Ocotillo and

The single red-breasted bird that sits at the very tip
of one of its branches.

I don't grab at endless ropes twisting
through my brain. It is too late for that,

Having been loved often and deeply.

If this is wisdom, a voice that says,
you don't have to grab at anything that
could destroy love,

So be it, that is wisdom.

I have an old friend who is dying
and I reach out to touch his disappearing,
red-breasted bird in flight.

Swami Rami

I once read of a Swami Rami
    who could sit
        on a dung heap
            at city's edge,
    while sitting there
        transform the air
            to a fragrance of flowers.

If inside our bodies we could visit Swami,
    sitting cross-legged
        under a kidney stone,
    we could ask his help to find
        our mounds of self-deception
            where love grieved
                and sometimes died.

And should his grace heal our eyes and hearts
    we may be moved to say,
        Yes, that mound is ours—and that one, too—
Amidst a scent of flowers.

Mostly Happy

I've been happy for a long time,
except there are pieces of me
    that don't know it
    and it's so hard
        to get their attention.

Forgery Expert

I have an agreement with God
    he may not have signed
No matter, over the years I have
    taught my faith
To become an expert at forgery

Amusement helps me bear
    the world's deception
When I pull out the document
    that signs me into heaven
The ache I carry
    in my stomach goes away

My abdomen
    is full of children
Who say they love me
    who signed on as witnesses

V

Love

You Are Not an Orphan

If you don't know where you came from
    dear one
It is not because you were once
    an orphan
It is because so many beautiful people
    dogs and other beings

loved you and you can't pull them
    apart enough to recognize
        every face

That gave you heart

My Father Headed In
—*for Norman Herbert Nickerson*

My weak and lame father
is building a head of steam
going into Summit tunnel,
an old engine dashing its last
miles into the yard of coupling

And uncoupling. He pulls a
line of empties, cattle cars and
flat cars. Memories blow past
him like tumbleweeds, rolling
up against a chicken wire fence.

Bawling white-faced calves
scrape down a chute to a white-
washed corral, a great belly-
engine hisses steam, and brown-
skin boys run to catch up to it.

My father's signals are fading,
like all the clapboard depots.
How soon must I invent sounds
I cannot hear, CHUGA chuga,
CHUGA chuga, working its way

Up the grade. I tell him, when you
reach the Summit, send me three
long blasts, sure as St. Mary's, so
I will hear them. Tap out a last word
from your key: I am here.

I have entered the yard.

Your Aging Face
—for Linda

Don't ask me to explain

why

I read

each new line on your face

as if

it were the beginning

of

a love letter

Blue Checkbook
—for my mother, Etzel Streif

One day I found my mother's worn
blue checkbooks and examined her

Scribbled notations on the stubs,
each one the same: Gvt. bond for

Don Lee, Gvt. bond for Don Lee.

I held up a checkbook and laughed.
Mother, I've got it! I've got it! I said.

You did what you could. You did what
you could. Then I laughed some more

and cried.

She called me Donnie all my life
and I hated it.

The Cheater

Love outweighs the ego
    on the scales of happiness
though the ego cheats
    with agile thumb

Wishing You Joy
—*for Katherine*

Others wish us happiness,
    success,
        long life and cheer,
I wish you joy instead. That and love.

Joy so elusive it can't be enthusiasm
    or optimism altogether,
        nor pretense that suffering
            does not exist.

Joy closer to delight,
    the way I remember you jumping up
    and down in the snow
        with a snowflake in your hand,
        watching it disappear,
            and not crying,
    delighting in the world, pain and all,
        in humans as they are,
        failings and all.

Joy I wish you, more of who you
    already are, smiles of affection over
        something small,
    your look of surprise that
        lights up your face.

Joy I wish you, and memories of our
    bonding times,
        something everlasting to
        carry in your heart
            like a tiny band of
                graceful mountain goats.

9/13/92 & 7/19/09

Speaking of Love

We could not speak of love
    if love did not exist
nor have the happiness of loving
    if at first it was not a gift

Waterfall and Pool
—for Karen

Sometimes I have many words,
    too many I believe
When my heart would prefer silence
    deeper than words,

Like a great pool where a waterfall
    splashes itself into joining waves,
Dancing foam, and at the edges of the
    pool tiny ripples from aeons ago.

You are a shimmering and cascading
    waterfall in the blue pool of my
Heart, at its edges lap memories from
    your very earliest years, streams

Traveling through my smiling mind,
    while at the pool's center
A place of continuous and powerful
    merging where you and I have

Always been connected
    indistinguishable
    one from the other.

11/3/04

Letter to Li Po

Your story is a bulging grapefruit,
and I linger over a late breakfast
savoring vignettes of your travels
between taverns and other sacred places.

You could climb to sit with monks
among green-hued clouds, or gaze out
to beautiful women from your swaying
river boat, it made no difference

where you came to be, each place
full as summer cherries,
while your poems came ruby ripe
off their rock-ribbed trees.

I will not grasp at your poems,
as if you could return at any moment
and cast them out to endless waters.
Instead, I will turn them over
in my mouth and long for
your graceful indifferences,

wondering if I am a sinner for
wanting our bellies to rub,
if it is too much to ask of you,
take my one poem in your light hands,
too much to want to hear the echo
of your laughter one more time.

Holiday

He welcomed death as if he were nodding
affirmatively to the offer
of a second piece of bacon.
He was fond of bacon
and often wondered
when the world would run out.

He was less taken by Christmas,
perhaps because he often felt left out.
He would sometimes stop his car
in front of one of the many worn
gray cottages with colored lights,
imagining what it might be like
to be invited in.

Aside from bacon and death,
he was inclined to like Carmina Burana.
He also leaned toward Easter,
the idea one might not be able
to get rid of love after all.

VI

For Fun

Hurryin' Up to Get My Beer

I like those trips
from the porch
        to the refrigerator,
makes me feel like I worked
    to get my beer,
        allows me to settle in
with the suds,
      oh, man, gotta' get me another can
      before the lady next door
        takes her dog out for a walk,
cute little thing,
    with curls,
           and a wiggle.

Dangerous Bridges

No sun has found a way to warn human flesh
how bridges across rivers behave just after dusk,
how they swallow station wagons
and unsuspecting college students on bikes.

It is the children peering out the windshield from the
back seat who see how headlights are falling on open jaws
and scream out their warnings,
but always too late.

Who could suspect, pondering the missing persons list,
that bridges in Wisconsin, Georgia, and other states
are responsible for so many deaths?

While detectives scan the muddy waters, leaning up
against the riveted rails,
the soaring steel arches above their shaking heads
effect a gray-whispered air of innocence.

General Arugula

General Arugula
    hides beneath a canopy of greens
        damp from curried olive oil,
  tosses off a warning
  from his friend, Raddicio,
      that expeditionary forks
      and spoons could soon invade.

No, said General Arugula,
    first they would have to pass through
    a field of scalloped Boston lettuce,
      sweet and hypnotic,
    after that, endive's edgy blades,
    and then the most dreaded foe of all,
      The Spinach Elite.

As a last resort, should all else fail,
    here, beneath the Sicilian olives
    and peppercorns, we will wait,
      like a Trojan horse wait for the
      silver fork to be lifted up,
        into their guarded citadel,
        past their ivory gates, past
          their gold and silver shields,

and onto their outstretched tongue.
Then we will strike,
unexpectedly, after they think
we are missing or dead.

Our men, on tiny stalks, will dash past their olfactory
outposts, leap over the epiglottis wall.
Our infantry will push up red ridges of the throat,
onto the sinus plateau. In a moment our target's
senses will be stunned,
he will be overcome, swoon, dream of nothing
but varieties of lettuce and herbs.

These humans, they will remember such a battle, Raddicio,
as they remember Waterloo or Lexington. They will learn
to say our names in the first year of school. At night,
when the light from a candle falls on a wooden bowl, flickers
over greens, they will say to their children,
Arugula, Raddicio, remember their names.

Postscript

During my late fifties, I was teaching a graduate counseling course in Gestalt Process and doing psychotherapy when I first began to write poetry and to read some Chinese poetry, which enchanted me. This process led to a class with Henry Carlile at Portland State University in Oregon, who was formative in my future writing for two reasons: he early on helped me recognize just how bad my poetry was, but he didn't get rid of me; and he referred me to poetry groups being taught by his then wife, Sandra McPherson, and Christopher Howell.

Whatever authentic poetic voice I have, for it I must for the most part give credit to these two exceptional teachers. I studied with them for years and cannot express my gratitude adequately for their giftedness. Because of their nature and generosity of spirit, I treasure the creative act of writing poetry more than any other feature of my life—even tennis!

I also wish to thank other poets who have given me their encouragement and support while I lived in Oregon, notably Verne Rutsala, who validated and supported my total body of work when I had no idea whether or not my poems warranted publishing; Peter Sears, who invited my collection of poems and came close to selecting some for his book on "Emerging Oregon Poets" (I was amused at the prospect of "emerging" at the age of 70!); Tom Crawford and Carlos Reyes for their teaching and encouragement; and two poets who, at one time, sat through many, many critiquing sessions with me, with either McPherson or Howell, Carolyn Miller and Lois Rosen.

As ever, I would like to thank my wife, Linda, for reading revision after revision of my poems and giving me her feedback on whether or not they were telling.

Finally, my heartfelt thanks to the SaddleBrooke Writer's Group for their support in the more than eight years I have belonged to this vital assembly. While not a critique group, at one time or another I read in their meetings a goodly number of the poems in this collection, and always felt their support and encouragement to write from my heart.

About the Author

Don L. Nickerson was born and grew up in the Mojave Desert in California, where his father worked as a station agent and telegrapher for the Santa Fe Railway. Some of these poems suggest the poet's affection for trains and travel. Other of his more recent poems reflect the spacious consciousness, even sacredness, he associates with the desert. Perhaps the majority speak of the heart, and the poet's embracing of many cultural, poetic, and spiritual traditions.

His most recent book of essays, *The Healing of Teddy Bears— Creating an Imaginative Faith*, was published in a revised version in 2008 by Wheatmark Publishing of Tucson, Arizona.

Both the Tucson Poetry Festival and the Southwestern Society of Authors have recognized his poems with awards.

Retired with his wife, Linda S. Larsen, to Tucson, Arizona, he is the father of four adult children. For comments he may be reached at lindontucson@aol.com.